My Year Plus Two

Weekly Planner 14 Month Edition

Activinotes

DAILY JOURNALS, PLANNERS, NOTEBOOKS AND OTHER BLANK BOOKS

Monthly Planner

January

MONDAY	TUESDAY	WEDNESDAY
THURSDAY	FRIDAY	SATURDAY

SUNDAY

MONDAY	TUESDAY	WEDNESDAY
THURSDAY	FRIDAY	SATURDAY

SUNDAY

Notes and Reminders

MONDAY	TUESDAY	WEDNESDAY
THURSDAY	FRIDAY	SATURDAY

SUNDAY

MONDAY	TUESDAY	WEDNESDAY
THURSDAY	FRIDAY	SATURDAY

SUNDAY

Notes and Reminders

Monthly Planner

Monthly Planner

February

MONDAY	TUESDAY	WEDNESDAY
THURSDAY	FRIDAY	SATURDAY

SUNDAY

MONDAY	TUESDAY	WEDNESDAY
THURSDAY	FRIDAY	SATURDAY

SUNDAY

Notes and Reminders

MONDAY	TUESDAY	WEDNESDAY
THURSDAY	FRIDAY	SATURDAY

SUNDAY

MONDAY	TUESDAY	WEDNESDAY
THURSDAY	FRIDAY	SATURDAY

SUNDAY

Notes and Reminders

Monthly Planner

Monthly Planner

March

MONDAY	TUESDAY	WEDNESDAY
THURSDAY	FRIDAY	SATURDAY

SUNDAY

MONDAY	TUESDAY	WEDNESDAY
THURSDAY	FRIDAY	SATURDAY

SUNDAY

Notes and Reminders

	MONDAY	TUESDAY	WEDNESDAY
	THURSDAY	FRIDAY	SATURDAY
SUNDAY			

	MONDAY	TUESDAY	WEDNESDAY
	THURSDAY	FRIDAY	SATURDAY
SUNDAY			

Notes and Reminders

Monthly Planner

Monthly Planner

April

MONDAY	TUESDAY	WEDNESDAY
THURSDAY	FRIDAY	SATURDAY

SUNDAY

MONDAY	TUESDAY	WEDNESDAY
THURSDAY	FRIDAY	SATURDAY

SUNDAY

Notes and Reminders

MONDAY	TUESDAY	WEDNESDAY
THURSDAY	FRIDAY	SATURDAY

SUNDAY

MONDAY	TUESDAY	WEDNESDAY
THURSDAY	FRIDAY	SATURDAY

SUNDAY

Notes and Reminders

Monthly Planner

Monthly Planner

May

MONDAY	TUESDAY	WEDNESDAY
THURSDAY	FRIDAY	SATURDAY

SUNDAY

MONDAY	TUESDAY	WEDNESDAY
THURSDAY	FRIDAY	SATURDAY

SUNDAY

Notes and Reminders

MONDAY	TUESDAY	WEDNESDAY
THURSDAY	FRIDAY	SATURDAY

SUNDAY

MONDAY	TUESDAY	WEDNESDAY
THURSDAY	FRIDAY	SATURDAY

SUNDAY

Notes and Reminders

Monthly Planner

Monthly Planner

June

MONDAY	TUESDAY	WEDNESDAY
THURSDAY	FRIDAY	SATURDAY

SUNDAY

MONDAY	TUESDAY	WEDNESDAY
THURSDAY	FRIDAY	SATURDAY

SUNDAY

Notes and Reminders

MONDAY	TUESDAY	WEDNESDAY

THURSDAY	FRIDAY	SATURDAY

SUNDAY

MONDAY	TUESDAY	WEDNESDAY

THURSDAY	FRIDAY	SATURDAY

SUNDAY

Notes and Reminders

Monthly Planner

Mid-Year Notes

Notes and Reminders

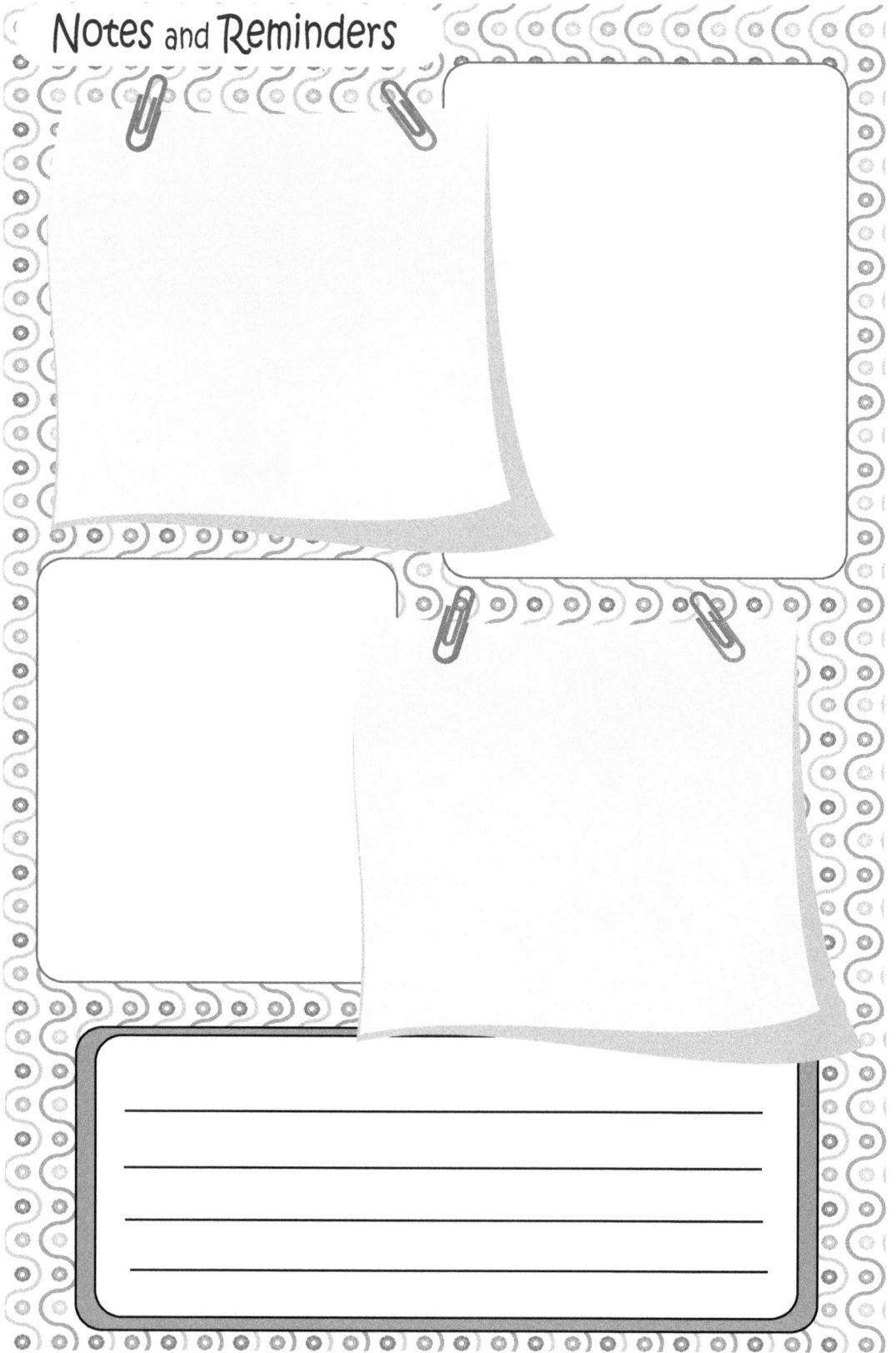

Notes and Reminders

Mid-Year Notes

Monthly Planner

July

MONDAY	TUESDAY	WEDNESDAY
THURSDAY	FRIDAY	SATURDAY

SUNDAY

MONDAY	TUESDAY	WEDNESDAY
THURSDAY	FRIDAY	SATURDAY

SUNDAY

Notes and Reminders

MONDAY	TUESDAY	WEDNESDAY
THURSDAY	FRIDAY	SATURDAY

SUNDAY

MONDAY	TUESDAY	WEDNESDAY
THURSDAY	FRIDAY	SATURDAY

SUNDAY

Notes and Reminders

Monthly Planner

Monthly Planner

August

MONDAY	TUESDAY	WEDNESDAY
THURSDAY	FRIDAY	SATURDAY

SUNDAY

MONDAY	TUESDAY	WEDNESDAY
THURSDAY	FRIDAY	SATURDAY

SUNDAY

Notes and Reminders

MONDAY	TUESDAY	WEDNESDAY
THURSDAY	FRIDAY	SATURDAY

SUNDAY

MONDAY	TUESDAY	WEDNESDAY
THURSDAY	FRIDAY	SATURDAY

SUNDAY

Notes and Reminders

Monthly Planner

Monthly Planner

September

MONDAY	TUESDAY	WEDNESDAY
THURSDAY	FRIDAY	SATURDAY
SUNDAY		

MONDAY	TUESDAY	WEDNESDAY
THURSDAY	FRIDAY	SATURDAY
SUNDAY		

Notes and Reminders

MONDAY	TUESDAY	WEDNESDAY
THURSDAY	FRIDAY	SATURDAY

SUNDAY

MONDAY	TUESDAY	WEDNESDAY
THURSDAY	FRIDAY	SATURDAY

SUNDAY

Notes and Reminders

Monthly Planner

Monthly Planner

October

MONDAY	TUESDAY	WEDNESDAY
THURSDAY	FRIDAY	SATURDAY

SUNDAY

MONDAY	TUESDAY	WEDNESDAY
THURSDAY	FRIDAY	SATURDAY

SUNDAY

Notes and Reminders

MONDAY	TUESDAY	WEDNESDAY
THURSDAY	FRIDAY	SATURDAY

SUNDAY

MONDAY	TUESDAY	WEDNESDAY
THURSDAY	FRIDAY	SATURDAY

SUNDAY

Notes and Reminders

Monthly Planner

Monthly Planner

November

MONDAY	TUESDAY	WEDNESDAY
THURSDAY	FRIDAY	SATURDAY

SUNDAY

MONDAY	TUESDAY	WEDNESDAY
THURSDAY	FRIDAY	SATURDAY

SUNDAY

Notes and Reminders

MONDAY	TUESDAY	WEDNESDAY
THURSDAY	FRIDAY	SATURDAY

SUNDAY

MONDAY	TUESDAY	WEDNESDAY
THURSDAY	FRIDAY	SATURDAY

SUNDAY

Notes and Reminders

Monthly Planner

Monthly Planner

December

MONDAY	TUESDAY	WEDNESDAY
THURSDAY	FRIDAY	SATURDAY

SUNDAY

MONDAY	TUESDAY	WEDNESDAY
THURSDAY	FRIDAY	SATURDAY

SUNDAY

Notes and Reminders

MONDAY	TUESDAY	WEDNESDAY

THURSDAY	FRIDAY	SATURDAY

SUNDAY

MONDAY	TUESDAY	WEDNESDAY

THURSDAY	FRIDAY	SATURDAY

SUNDAY

Notes and Reminders

Monthly Planner

Birthday Reminder

Birthday Reminder

January

Birthday Reminder

February

Birthday Reminder

March

Birthday Reminder

April

Birthday Reminder

May

Birthday Reminder

June

Birthday Reminder

July

Birthday Reminder

August

Birthday Reminder

September

Birthday Reminder

October

Birthday Reminder

November

Birthday Reminder

December

Notes and Reminders

Monthly Planner

January

MONDAY	TUESDAY	WEDNESDAY
THURSDAY	FRIDAY	SATURDAY

SUNDAY

MONDAY	TUESDAY	WEDNESDAY
THURSDAY	FRIDAY	SATURDAY

SUNDAY

Notes and Reminders

MONDAY	TUESDAY	WEDNESDAY
THURSDAY	FRIDAY	SATURDAY

SUNDAY

MONDAY	TUESDAY	WEDNESDAY
THURSDAY	FRIDAY	SATURDAY

SUNDAY

Notes and Reminders

Monthly Planner

Monthly Planner

February

MONDAY	TUESDAY	WEDNESDAY
THURSDAY	FRIDAY	SATURDAY

SUNDAY

MONDAY	TUESDAY	WEDNESDAY
THURSDAY	FRIDAY	SATURDAY

SUNDAY

Notes and Reminders

MONDAY	TUESDAY	WEDNESDAY

THURSDAY	FRIDAY	SATURDAY

SUNDAY

MONDAY	TUESDAY	WEDNESDAY

THURSDAY	FRIDAY	SATURDAY

SUNDAY

Notes and Reminders

Monthly Planner

Notes

www.ingramcontent.com/pod-product-compliance
Lightning Source LLC
Chambersburg PA
CBHW081335090426
42737CB00017B/3153